Tatsuki Fujimoto

I love *The Menu*!

Tatsuki Fujimoto won Honorable Mention in the
November 2013 Shueisha Crown Newcomers' Awards for
his debut one-shot story "Love Is Blind." His first series,
Fire Punch, ran for eight volumes. *Chainsaw Man* began
serialization in 2018 in *Weekly Shonen Jump*.

15

SHONEN JUMP Edition

Story & Art TATSUKI FUJIMOTO

Translation/AMANDA HALEY
Touch-Up Art & Lettering/SABRINA HEEP
Design/JULIAN [JR] ROBINSON
Editor/ALEXIS KIRSCH

CHAINSAW MAN © 2018 by Tatsuki Fujimoto
All rights reserved.
First published in Japan in 2018 by SHUEISHA Inc., Tokyo.
English translation rights arranged by SHUEISHA Inc.

The stories, characters, and incidents mentioned in this publication are
entirely fictional.

Printed in the U.S.A.

Published by VIZ Media, LLC
P.O. Box 77010
San Francisco, CA 94107

10 9 8 7 6 5 4 3 2 1
First printing, May 2024

CHAINSAWMAN

15

Hors D'oeuvre

Tatsuki Fujimoto

CHARACTERS

Asa Mitaka

A lonely, bullied young woman who doesn't fit in at school. She was killed by the Justice Devil, but came back to life when the War Devil, Yoru, took over her body. Asa hates devils—they killed her parents—and she's no fan of Chainsaw Man either. Her current battle? Handling Yoru!!

Yoru (War Devil)

This War Devil's true form is owllike, but she hopped into Asa's body and claimed half of the human's brain. See, she's on a mission to kill Chainsaw Man...but if she wants to track him down, she'll need help blending into human society. She has the power to transform things she kills into weapons.

Denji (Chainsaw Man)

Chainsaw Man! He carries the Chainsaw Devil in his heart (literally). High schooler by day, vigilante devil hunter by night. Kishibe from Public Safety entrusted him with the new Control Devil, Nayuta...

Fami (The Famine Devil)

A mysterious member of the devil hunter club at Asa's school. She's the sister of the War Devil.

Hirofumi Yoshida

A devil hunter who belongs to a particular organization. Wants to keep Denji's identity under wraps.

STORY

Asa Mitaka is a lonely young woman who doesn't fit in at school. Even the class president, the closest person she has to a friend, hates Asa so much that she makes a contract with the Justice Devil and murders her. But that's when the War Devil, Yoru, takes over Asa's body, giving her a second chance at life! Yoru's on a mission to find Chainsaw Man, and she claims she'll return Asa's body if they can kill him...

In order to turn Denji into a weapon, Asa asks him out on a date at the aquarium. However, due to the Eternity Devil sent by Fami, Asa, Denji, Yoshida, and others become trapped there. While things start looking grim, Asa is able to turn the situation around with some quick thinking. Afterward, Asa tries to become closer with Denji, but her failure at human interaction causes her to despair.

Meanwhile, Fami tells Yoshida of the terrible fate that is about to befall the world. And at the same time, a terrifying primal devil makes its appearance...

CONTENTS

Chapter 123: Hors D'oeuvre

OH... OH?

... DEAR.

WO OO

I'M BEING QUITE INDECENT.

ASA! SNAP OUT OF IT!

THAT DEVIL'S POWER IS CAUSING YOUR NEGATIVE FEELINGS!

NOW THEN, ALLOW ME TO BEGIN COOKING.

...MY HORS D'OEUVRE, LA ROOT VONLA.

FOR THE FIRST COURSE, IT WILL BE MY PLEASURE TO FEED YOU...

OF THE TWO OF US, ONLY YOU CAN CREATE STRONG WEAPONS!

ARE YOU LISTEN-ING?!

CLAP

WHAT IS IT, MA'AM?

ASA, CAN WE TALK?

WHY DON'T WE HAVE MY FRIEND WHO LIKES CATS TAKE HIM?

IT'S ABOUT YOUR CAT.

ONE OF THE OTHER KIDS IS ALLERGIC.

HUH?

THIS IS UNHEALTHY FOR YOU TOO. YOU DEPEND ON THAT CAT'S COMPANIONSHIP INSTEAD OF INTERACTING WITH OTHER PEOPLE.

MAY THE FLAVOR OF PAST TRAUMAS DELIGHT YOUR TASTE BUDS.

THE LOWER THE HEART SINKS, THE HIGHER THE BODY FALLS. THAT'S THE CONCEPT OF THIS DISH.

creak

ASA! I CAN'T ENTER YOUR BODY!!

DON'T BE AFRAID!!

Chapter 124: Soup

THUMP

ASA, YOU FOCUS ON THE PAIN IN YOUR FINGER.

IT'LL KEEP YOUR FEAR AT BAY.

I STILL FALL DOWN-WARD... THOUGHT SO.

NO, THIS DEVIL MAKES YOUR HAIR STAND ON END.

THE FEAR IS MORE PRIMAL THAN THAT.

GRAVITY.

THE DEVIL'S NAME IS... TRAUMA.

SUICIDE...

MOON...

A TRAUMATIC FLASHBACK, FOLLOWED BY...

SOME OF THE HUMANS ARE UNAFFECTED.

...RE-VERSED GRAVITY?

FALLING?

OR FAMINE'S INTERFERENCE AGAIN?

WHY DID SHE APPEAR HERE?

IS IT COINCIDENCE?

OWWW!!

ONLY
THINK
ABOUT
THE PAIN.
UNDER-
STAND?

IT
HURTS,
NO?

THAT
HURTS.

I'M DESPERATELY TRYING TO KEEP YOUR BODY ALIVE HERE!!

WHY FEAR ME *NOW*?!

YOU'RE AFRAID OF ME!!

YOU DROVE ME OUT OF YOUR BODY AGAIN!!

TRUST ME, YOU IDIOT !!

STUPID ?!

TRUST YOU?!

HOW CAN I, STUPID?!

WITH MY AGILITY, WE MIGHT ESCAPE.

YOUR FEAR JEOPARDIZES YOUR SURVIVAL.

THE DEVIL'S POWER IS MAKING YOU NEGATIVE.

THINK THIS THROUGH RATIONALLY.

YOU CAN LOOK INSIDE MY MIND AND SEE, RIGHT...?

WHAT I'M REALLY AFRAID OF.

I HAVE TRUST ISSUES, BUT I'M LONELY...

...SO ONCE IN A WHILE I'LL APPROACH SOMEONE...

...BUT SOMETHING *ALWAYS* GOES WRONG...

...AND I GET HURT...

...AND THEN I WIND UP ALL ALONE AGAIN!

SOLITUDE AND COMPANION-SHIP...

I'M AFRAID OF *BOTH!*

MNGH! MNGH!

A POTAGE MADE FROM THE EARS, TONGUE, AND NOSE OF A DEVIL HUNTER WHO TRIED TO HUNT ME.

FOR THE SOUP COURSE, I PRESENT *DE ROOT ATELANTA.*

Supermarket
AJI

Fruits, Veggies, Meat

TEN EYES.

FOUR EARS.

THAT LEAVES ...

EXCUSE ME, DO YOU HAVE AN APPLE VARIETY THAT PAIRS WELL WITH HUMAN FLESH?

NOW, ABOUT THOSE APPLES ...

OH DEAR. PLEASE, RELAX.

UNLESS YOU ATTACK ME FIRST, I MEAN YOU NO HARM.

I'M SHORRY... I'M SHORRY...

THE RECIPE FOR THE SAUCE CALLED FOR A MAN'S HEAD.

GOODNESS, ME. I FORGOT.

EXCUSE ME, COULD SOMEBODY SPARE ME ONE?

BANG BANG
BANG BANG
BANG

BANG

BANG

CEASE
FIRE.

BANG

...AND THEN I'LL TAKE MY LEAVE.

MY FINAL TASK IS TO DROP ASA MITAKA INTO HELL...

I WON'T KILL ANY MORE HUMANS. THERE'S NO NEED FOR US TO FIGHT.

YOU MUST BE CHAIN-SAW MAN.

DID YOU SAY...

...DROP ASA MITAKA INTO HELL?

THAT'S RIGHT.

GYAAA-
AAAH?!

I DETEST UGLI-NESS.

...CHAINSAW MAN.

I STILL NEED YOU TO FIGHT...

ASA!

GNNGH!

creak

WHAT TRULY SCARES YOU RIGHT NOW IS THE SHOCK OF THE IMPACT.

THE DARKNESS OF THE SKY. THAT'S ALL.

THE PHYSICAL SENSATION OF FALLING.

I CAN TELL BY THE WAY YOUR MUSCLES MOVE. BY THE SMELL OF YOUR SWEAT.

YOUR ATTACH-MENT TO LIFE IS WEAK TO BEGIN WITH, NO?

CLOSE YOUR EYES...

...AND I CAN PROMISE YOU A PEACEFUL FALL.

I WON'T HAVE TO CAUSE TROUBLE FOR ANYONE ELSE...

OH...

....OR GET MY FEELINGS HURT ANYMORE.

BUT I DO HAVE ONE REGRET.

I WON'T HAVE TO LIE IN BED...

EVEN ONE PERSON...

EVEN IF IT WAS WITH ONLY ONE PERSON, WITH ALL MY HEART, I WISH I'D...

...THINKING ABOUT ALL THE THINGS I DID WRONG AS I WAIT TO FALL ASLEEP.

Ice
cream!
Ice
cream!

We
stopped!
Cats!
Cats!

NNNNNGH
...!

UHN!
UHHHN...!

DON'T MAKE ME REMEM-BER CATS!

NO ONE HAS IT WORSE THAN ME!!

WHAT WOULD YOU KNOW ?!

BELIEVE ME, I'VE BEEN THERE!!

I KNOW HOW YOU FEEL!!

JUST WHEN LIFE SEEMS SUPER AWESOME, AS SOON AS YOU LET YOUR GUARD DOWN...

...SOME CRAPPY THING HAPPENS OUTTA NOWHERE AND SCREWS IT ALL UP, RIGHT?!

YOU KNOW LIFE ISN'T **ALL** BAD...

...BUT DAY IN AND DAY OUT, ALL YOU CAN REMEMBER IS THE BAD STUFF...

...AND THE DISASTERS KEEP PILIN' UP LIKE A HAMBURGER MADE OF CRAP, RIGHT?

I'm NOT OVER IT!

I HAVEN'T!

...CHAIN-SAW MAN?

HOW DID YOU GET OVER THAT...

WHAT'S THAT?

ONLY...

...I'VE GOT SOMETHING TO LIVE FOR! SOMETHING I LOOK FORWARD TO SO MUCH THAT I'M WILLING TO EAT THAT CRAPBURGER!

GROSS! YOU'RE A CREEP!

I CHANGED MY MIND! FORGET IT! GO TO HELL!!

THINK ABOUT IT! HUMANITY GREW TO THIS SIZE CUZ SEX FEELS SO DAMN GOOD!

WE'RE BOTH HERE NOW CUZ OF THE POWER OF SEX TOO!!

HUH?! IT'S NOT GROSS!!

Sex is, like, super beautiful!

LIKE, SOMEBODY ELSE'S SALIVA AND SWEAT ALL MIXING TOGETHER WITH YOURS?! IT'S JUST GROSS!!

PEOPLE ONLY HAVE SEX BECAUSE THEY HAVE NOTHING BETTER TO DO!!

Chapter 128: Main Dish

ARE YOU FOR REAL RIGHT NOW?!

NOTHING'S BETTER THAN SOMEBODY'S SALIVA AND SWEAT MIXING WITH YOURS!!

WAIT... HUH?

WAIT A SEC. WHAT MAKES YOU EVEN THINK *YOU* WOULD EVER GET ANY?

EVEN IF I CAN'T GET ANY RIGHT NOW...

...WHEN I'M OLDER, I'LL EVENTU-ALLY GET A GIRLFRIEND, AND THEN...

HUH? ARE YOU FOR *REAL*?

WHAP

THE FALLING DEVIL HAS NO TOLERANCE FOR DINERS WHO LEAVE THEIR FOOD UNFINISHED.

THEY'LL DESPERATELY TRY TO DEVOUR ASA MITAKA, LEST THEY BE KILLED BY THE FALLING DEVIL.

Chain saw man

...CHAIN-
SAW
MANS?

TWO...

FINISH HIM WHILE HE'S DOWN!!

ASA! NOW'S OUR CHANCE!

GAH!

GHK!

YOU
ALWAYS
DO THIS!

WHY...

...MUST
YOU ALWAYS
DO THE
OPPOSITE
OF WHAT
I SAY?!

grab

wHA

M

OWWW
?!

drip

...CHAIN-SAW MAN HAS SAVED MY LIFE TWICE NOW!

BETWEEN THAT TIME WITH YUKO AND TONIGHT...

YOU DON'T HAVE TO TAKE IT SO FAR AS TO SAVE MY MORTAL ENEMY!!

YOU'RE CROSS-ING THE LINE!!

BESIDES, WATCHING CHAINSAW MAN MAKES ME THINK...

...IF A PIECE OF TRASH LIKE HIM IS ALLOWED TO KEEP LIVING...

...THEN MAYBE IT'S OKAY FOR *ME* TO LIVE TOO!

THAT'S WHY—

ASA!!

HOW IS THE TASTE...

...OF HUMAN STEEPED IN FEAR?

I MADE
THAT
MEAL
WITH
LOVE...

I...
I MUH—

BLR

...THROW
IT
UP?!

HOW
DARE
YOU...

I CONTROLLED THAT DEVIL'S BRAIN A TEENSY BIT...

CONTROL.

...TO MAKE HUMANS TASTE LIKE LITERAL CRAP.

WHY ARE YOU AFTER DENJI AND THIS GIRL...

...SIS?

NOSTRADA-MUS'S PROPHECY IS COMING TRUE.

THE ULTIMATE TERROR WILL SOON DESCEND ON THIS WORLD.

WHAT?! No more pizza?!

No way!

...THINGS LIKE PIZZA AND CHINESE FOOD WILL CEASE TO BE.

IF AN AGE OF DEVILS COMES...

IT'S THE WORST SCENARIO IMAGINABLE.

I KNOW.

...NOR CHAINSAW MAN WILL BE ABLE TO STOP THE PROPHECY.

...NOR YOU...

AT THIS RATE, NEITHER I...

BUT...

...WAR DEVIL COULD...

...BE MADE TO WIN...

---POSSIBLY.

WORK WITH ME, CONTROL.

YOU JUST TRIED TO KILL HER!

WHAT GIVES?!

MY INTENTION WAS ONLY TO STARVE WAR IN THAT DEVIL'S BELLY.

WITH OUR STRENGTH COMBINED, THE AGE OF DEVILS MAY NOT ARRIVE.

I CAN TURN THE STARVED INTO MY PAWNS.

WHY NOT?

No way!

CUZ I HAVE SCHOOL!

Chapter 132: Protection

SHOTA, YUMI.

GIMME YOUR DESSERTS.

'KAY.

HERE.

MIU DIED TOO...

SHE'S MISSING, YOU MEAN!

LIKE, MORE KIDS ARE PROBABLY DEAD THAN ARE MOVING, DON'T YOU THINK?

IS IT JUST ME OR ARE A LOT OF KIDS ABSENT TODAY?

I HEARD A LOT OF PEOPLE ARE MOVING AWAY FROM TOKYO.

DASH

OH REALLY ...

Power outages continue to affect all districts of the Tokyo Metropolitan area...

...with planned blackouts scheduled for the districts above.

Report any persons inciting fear during the confusion to this number...

At this time, confirmed casualties and missing persons exceed 2,000.

EXCUSE MEEE!!

THOSE WHO ARE SEATED, PLEASE MAKE WAY!!

MAKE WAY, PLEASE!!

AH!

EXCUSE ME! COMING THROUGH!

MY GRAND-KID ABOUT YOUR AGE...

...GOT CRUSHED BY DEBRIS...

CHAINSAW MAN... SAVED ME AGAIN...

MAKE WAAAY!

THE CHAINSAW MAN CHURCH IS NOW RECRUITING TALENT TO FIGHT ALONGSIDE CHAINSAW MAN!

THE CHAINSAW MAN CHURCH FOR WORLD PEACE!

HELP US PREVENT THE COMING PROPHECY OF NOSTRA-DAMUS!

FIGHT WITH US AT THE FORE-FRONT!

WHOOO!!

OH! PEACE!

FAMI!

DID I REALLY HAVE TO APPEAR ON THAT LOWBROW VARIETY SHOW?!

DAMMIT!!

THEY SPUN MY EVERY WORD INTO MATERIAL FOR THE HOST'S JOKES!!

WHY?!

RELAX.

YOU DON'T NEED TO THINK.

THE RIDICULE WAS THE POINT.

YOUR JOB IS TO BE THE FACE.

FAMI IS THE BRAINS.

TOGETHER, YOU MOVE THE BODY— THE CHAINSAW MAN CHURCH.

IT'S LIKE FAMI SAYS.

...WALK TOWARD A WORLD WITHOUT EVIL, AREN'T YOU?

AND WITH THAT BODY, YOU'RE GONNA...

IT'S ALL FOR CHAINSAW MAN'S SAKE...

YES... I KNOW...

GOSH, THIS IS A RELIEF, DENJI.

YOU CALL THIS PROTECTION? FALLING ASLEEP IN CLASS ONLY TO WAKE UP TIED TO SOME CHAIR?

I'M GLAD I GOT YOU TO PROTECTION SAFE AND SOUND.

THEY SAID HER INJURIES ARE MINOR.

ASA MITAKA IS IN THE HOSPITAL.

WHAT ABOUT THE DOGS?

WHERE'S NAYUTA?

WE WON'T HARM NAYUTA OR THE DOGS.

NO TONGUING NECESSARY.

GO TO HELL!!

NOT WHILE YOU'RE UNDER OUR PROTECTION, ANYWAY.

Chain saw man

OH!

BECAUSE THEY DON'T LIKE YOU.

BUT WHY? I'M A GOOD BOY.

THOSE GUYS CLASHING WITH THE PROTESTORS ARE FOLLOWERS OF THAT CHAINSAW MAN CHURCH THING, RIGHT?

BECAUSE THEY LIKE YOU.

WHY ARE THEY FIGHTING THE PROTESTORS?

...HAVIN' PEOPLE FIGHT OVER ME.

FEELS KINDA NICE...

RECENTLY, THOUGH, INCREASING NUMBERS OF YOUNG PEOPLE ARE JOINING JUST FOR THE HELL OF IT. I'M TOLD MEMBERSHIP NOW EXCEEDS 20,000.

BEFORE, THE CHAINSAW MAN CHURCH CONSISTED LARGELY OF YOUR FANS AND DEVIL VICTIMS.

APPARENTLY POLITICIANS ARE ALREADY STARTING TO CONTRIBUTE SUPPLIES TO THE CHURCH TOO.

THE BULK OF THEM ARE STILL IN SCHOOL, BUT EVENTUALLY, THEY'LL BE OLD ENOUGH TO VOTE.

HOPEFULLY IT WILL STOP AT THESE SMALLER PROTESTS, BUT THERE IS A CHANCE OF CHAINSAW MANIA EVOLVING INTO A LARGER CONFLICT.

YOU NO LONGER HAVE SOLE CONTROL OVER CHAINSAW MAN.

WHAT'S THAT MEAN?

I WANT YOU TO DO ABSOLUTELY NOTHING.

AND? WHAT DO I GOTTA DO TO SEE NAYUTA AND THE DOGS?

I'M ASKING YOU TO NEVER TRANSFORM INTO CHAINSAW MAN AGAIN.

HELL, NO.

I HEARD THAT YOU LONG TO LIVE A NORMAL LIFE.

...WITH NAYUTA AT YOUR SIDE.

SIMPLY STOP TRANS- FORMING, AND THAT DREAM COMES TRUE...

THIS IS YOUR CHANCE TO BE HUMAN AGAIN, DENJI.

I...!
I WANT
PEOPLE
TO FIGHT
PROTESTORS
FOR ME!!

I DON'T
WANT
THAT
EITHER!

LOOK,
DENJI...

THE TIME
HAS COME
FOR YOU TO
CHOOSE...

...
BETWEEN
NAYUTA'S
LIFE...

...AND
YOUR
GREEDY
DESIRES.

BUT I
ALSO DON'T
WANNA
STOP BEING
CHAINSAW
MAN!!

DON'T YOU CARE IF NAYUTA DIES?!

PROTES-TORS, assemble!!

KILL THIS GUY FOR ME!!

DEN-JIII!!

HE'S EVEN DUMBER THAN I THOUGHT!

NAYUTA
!!

Denji
!!

HUH? YOU WEREN'T DONE YET?

IT'S TOO SOON TO LET THEM MEET!!

YOU STINK!

CUZ I HAVEN'T HAD A BATH!

LISTEN TO ME, DENJI!!

YOU WERE ABOUT TO CHOOSE NAYUTA'S LIFE AND GET SENT HOME TOGETHER!

WHY ...?!

EX-CUSE ME?!

Denji! Tell this guy to eff off!!

Now!!

WHATEVER! THIS MUST HAVE PROVEN IT TO YOU!

IF YOU TURN INTO CHAINSAW MAN, PUBLIC SAFETY **WILL** KILL NAYUTA!!

YOU DONE?! THEN WE'RE GOIN' HOME!

DID HE NOT UNDER-STAND ME?

TO BE CONTINUED...

CHAINSAW
MAN

Variety Show

OH...
THAT GIRL
WHO JUST
APPEARED
ON THE
SHOW IS
REALLY
CUTE...

WELL...
IF I LEARNED
SOME MAKEUP
TRICKS AND WORKED
ON MY HAIR,
I COULD PROBABLY
SURPASS HER.

BUT THAT'S A
LOT OF WORK,
AND IT'S NOT
LIKE I WANT
TO BE CUTE.
SO, IT'S NOT
BECAUSE I CAN'T,
I JUST DON'T
WANT TO.

THAT GIRL'S
ONLY ATTRIBUTE
IS BEING CUTE,
BUT I'M ALSO
PRETTY SMART.
SO OVERALL,
I'M AHEAD
OF HER.

Movie

THIS ACTRESS IS REALLY GOOD...

WAIT... BUT BEING A GOOD ACTRESS MEANS YOU'RE A GOOD LIAR. SO THAT'S NOT REALLY A GOOD THING FOR YOUR EVERYDAY LIFE...

IF I PRACTICED REALLY HARD, I COULD PROBABLY BECOME AN ACTRESS, BUT I DON'T WANT TO BECAUSE I AM AGAINST LYING... THOUGH IF SOMEONE OFFERED ME A JOB, I MIGHT DO IT...

DO YOU EVER SHUT UP?

THE CELEBRITY LIFESTYLE CAN REALLY MESS YOU UP, SO I PROBABLY HAVE AN OVERALL BETTER LIFE THAN HER. SO, I'M GLAD I'VE NEVER BEEN APPROACHED ON THE STREET BY SCOUTS. THOUGH IF I DID BECOME AN ACTRESS, OVERALL, I WOULD BE...

YOU'RE READING THE WRONG WAY!

Chainsaw Man reads from right to left, starting in the upper-right corner. Japanese is read from right to left, meaning that action, sound effects, and word-balloon order are completely reversed from English order.